YESTERDAY, TODAY, FOREVER . . .

Jesus

written by

Bruce Marchiano

HARVEST HOUSE
PUBLISHERS
EUGENE, OREGON

Visual Entertainment, Inc.
Dallas, Texas

Visual Entertainment, Inc.
16475 Dallas Parkway, Suite 790
Dallas, Texas 75248

Design and production by Koechel Peterson & Associates, Minneapolis, Minnesota

JESUS
Copyright © 1999 by Bruce Marchiano
Published by Harvest House Publishers, Eugene, Oregon 97402
and Visual Entertainment, Dallas, Texas 75248

Library of Congress Cataloging-in-Publication Data

Marchiano, Bruce.
    Jesus / Bruce Marchiano.
        p.   cm.
   ISBN 0-7369-0048-9
   1. Jesus Christ—Biography Devotional literature.   2. Christian
life.   I. Title.
BT306.5.M26   1999
232.9'01—dc21
[B]   99-21981
                                            CIP

Printed in Hong Kong.
99 00 01 02 03 04 05 06 07 08 / NG / 10 9 8 7 6 5 4 3 2 1

Taking the five loaves and

the two fish and looking up to heaven,

He gave thanks . . .

In the pages that follow, what began as "five loaves and two fish" became multiplied and multiplied through the committed hands, open hearts, and encouragement of many talented people: Robby Botha, whose respect and sensitivity gave me the confidence to open my heart in front of his camera lens. Regardt van den Bergh, whose direction and commitment to God's leading no matter the personal risk opened the doors for a fresh revelation of Jesus Christ. Harvest House Publishers and David Siebert of Visual Entertainment, who trusted me creatively. Barbara Sherrill, whose flexible hands gave opportunity for the book to grow and develop far beyond what any of us dreamed. Betty Fletcher—the most "beyond the beyond" editor a guy could hope for—who so gracefully allowed rules to be broken and lines to be redrawn so that lives would be changed. Jon Godfredson, whose skill as a designer was topped only by his patience in our relentless pursuit of something special. Julie McKinney, who believed as no one believed and whose ninth-inning touches when I was too tired to step up to the plate took this book to a level that astounds me. Bruce Rudnick, whose walk with God takes my breath away. Dad and Mom, who kept me in food and clothing through those 14-hours-a-day, seven-days-a-week writing stretches. The people from all over the world—most specifically South Africa and the United States—through whose daily prayers and letters the Lord whispers in those tired and questioning moments, "Keep going, kid. You're doin' good." And of course, almighty God, who has unveiled before me one excitement after another, who revealed things in the writing of this book that I'd never considered until I read it back to myself, who gave me a life when I had none, and through whose hands I am humbly confident that the miracle of the loaves and fishes will here be repeated in lives untold.

To our God and Father

be all the glory for ever and ever!

Jesus—Y'shua, Joshua, Jesu, Aisau . . . the name carries the same magnificent meaning no matter what tongue or language, ancient or contemporary: "God Saves."

What an astounding truth! Can you imagine what it might have been like 2000 years ago to look into salvation's human eyes—the eyes of Jesus? It must have poured from His every glance, pulsated from His every touch, exploded from His every smile, every tear: "He saves; He saves; He saves . . ."

As an actor a handful of years ago, I enjoyed the rare and humbling honor of portraying Jesus in the Visual Bible film production *The Gospel According to Matthew.* Every day of filming was an experience beyond the extraordinary, revealing more and more, deeper and deeper, a Man beyond the extraordinary.

Alongside me on that adventure was a film-set photographer Robby Botha. Tiptoeing in the background with a huge telephoto lens cradled against his eagle eye, Robby snapped scores of frames a day, quietly recording every "Jesus" moment.

Schooled by years as a South African photojournalist, Robby was skilled beyond skilled in his eye for documentary reality, in the ability to capture on film that specific encounter, that specific look in the eye that captures the whole story or in this case, the story of stories—Jesus.

Though it may be bold to say, I believe Robby was handpicked and ordained by Father God for the purpose of capturing the essence of His beloved Son in still photography, and it is my absolute thrill to team with him in the pages that follow for that breathtakingly holy purpose.

When we began filming *Matthew*, the Lord gave director Regardt van den Bergh a promise. It's Isaiah 25:6-9, and it goes like this:

On this mountain the Lord Almighty will prepare a feast of rich food for all peoples, a banquet of aged wine—the best of meats and the finest of wines. On this mountain He will destroy the shroud that enfolds all peoples, the sheet that covers all nations; He will swallow up death forever. The Sovereign Lord will wipe away the tears from all faces; He will remove the disgrace of His people from all the earth. The Lord has spoken. In that day they will say, "Surely this is our God; we trusted in Him and He saved us. This is the Lord, we trusted in Him; let us rejoice and be glad in His salvation."

And to quote Regardt with regard to that promise, "Rejoice and be glad! Rejoice and be glad! I pray the Lord will impart to your spirit His wondrous reality as seen through the eyes of our wondrous experience. That the joy of Jesus will be multiplied to your soul, that you may live in that 'perfect law of liberty.' "

So come with us now! Let your imagination wander back a couple thousand years. Hear the shofar's trumpet call to worship echoing across the hills and valleys of ancient Israel.

There's talk of a new prophet, you know—a carpenter from the town of Nazareth in Galilee. It is said He speaks with truth and acts with compassion such as no one has ever seen before.

Come! Stand in the temple courts with Him, share a meal by His campfire. Laugh with Him, weep with Him. Look into His eyes, feel the warmth of His embrace, peek into His heart, and glimpse the salvation of your very soul—

Jesus

A CHILD

So are My ways higher than your ways . . .

One

What kind of God would choose to be born in a barn—a barn in one of the tiniest little burgs in the ancient world? What kind of God would choose a peasant girl for His mother and a no-name blue-collar worker for His father? What kind of God would choose a feed trough as His first resting place, farm animals as His first companions?

We've done a good job of hiding the realities behind the romance of Christmas pageantry and celebration—all done, surely, with a heart to glorify the Lord we love so much. But to step away from those glittering nativity scenes, peel the poetry from those timeless carols, and stare into the face of unaltered, unglamorized, unreligionized truth is to look into the face and glimpse the pulsating heart of almighty God Himself.

···———◉———···

What was it like that night 2000 years ago—what was it really like?

I think of Mary, this woman—possibly this girl—eight-plus months pregnant on the back of a donkey (if she and Joseph even had a donkey); dirt roads; mountain passes; sun, wind, cold; no shelter, no escape; just miles, miles, and more miles; pain, pain, and more pain.

Less than a year before, she had been surrounded by family, laughing with friends in the streets of her beloved Nazareth, a young woman betrothed to a gentle, godly man with a good trade, the whole world lying at her feet. And now, here she is, a nameless face in the throng of oppressed migration, trekking across merciless terrain, alone except for the kick in her belly, a man as worn as she is, and a promise that the tiny heartbeat within her is that of the Son of the Living God.

I think of the sweat dripping down her face, the trail-dust clinging to her clothes, the pregnant swell of her feet and limbs, the endless pounding of every step. I think of her curled up by the night's campfire, bundled against the cold, her mind and emotions racing: "Surely this is not the way a king is born into the world, let alone Messiah. This is not glory. This is not majesty. Did I hear the angel correctly? But I am pregnant, and there's no other way. It has to be true . . . help me, Lord, it hurts!"

What kind of God

would choose a feed

trough as His first

resting place, farm

animals as His first

companions?

A child is born . . .

Yes, I know we have greatly idealized Mary, but the truth is she was a woman—a woman with one tremendous asset: a heart after God. But at the same time, she was a woman no less subject to the same doubt, confusion, fatigue, and fear as any other woman. A woman who had the same choice to make as any other woman: Am I going to walk this day God's way or my own? Am I going to trust Him—that He is who He says He is, and that His promises are true against all evidence to the contrary—or am I not?

And then there's her betrothed, Joseph. A man. Good-hearted, compassionate, and no doubt going through the same confusion as Mary, asking himself the very same questions.

I can't help but picture the two of them lying side by side next to that campfire, both shaking scared, both doing their best to hide it and be strong for the other. I imagine them having that standard exchange which has been going on between couples since the beginning of time: "Are you okay?" "Yeah, I'm fine." "Are you sure?" "No, really, I'm fine . . . How about you?" "Doin' just fine. Really . . ."

All humor aside, think of Joseph the man. His was a very real, day-by-day life 2000 years ago. We tend to overlook that in our hunt through the Gospels for great spiritual truth; we overlook the humanity, the dirt under the fingernails, the wrinkles on the forehead, the struggle to make ends meet. And in doing that we overlook what could possibly be the most significant truth of all: These were people 2000 years ago—very real, very human, very-much-like-you-and-I *people.*

And while they were "chosen" people, their chosenness had nothing to do with them being special people but everything to do with them being *yielded* people; chosen, not to live high and bask in God's favor, but chosen to serve (yes, this is the glory of God: to serve!), chosen to be a conduit through which the love of God and the plan of His salvation would flow, starting with the guy next door and to the very ends of the earth!

Try, for a moment, to put yourself in this man Joseph's shoes. Try to imagine that day he went home to his father and announced, "Mary's pregnant, but I'm going to marry her anyway because an angel told me the baby is Messiah!" Imagine, further, the day he announced it to his friends. I wasn't there, but I have to believe that each and every one of them looked straight at him and thought the exact same thought: *Joseph's gone nuts!*

Am I going to trust Him—that He is who He says He is, and that His promises are true against all evidence to the contrary— or am I not?

I can hear his father exploding in a righteous rage, "Over my dead body, you'll marry her!" I can see his buddies sitting him down a bit more calmly: "I know she's a great girl and all, but the woman's pregnant, pal. How do you think she got that way? Open your eyes. Walk away."

And you know, Joseph's dad and buddies would have had every right to react that way, assuming that's the way they reacted. A woman pregnant out of wedlock! It would have been blatantly horrifying to their first-century culture, not to mention a crime so grievous under the law of Moses that it was punishable by death.

How could Yahweh possibly, in His ultimate holiness and purity, choose to birth His Messiah in such an apparently unholy and impure arena? To our oh-so-familiar-with-the-story hindsight, the incongruity rarely even crosses the mind, but to them on that day it would have made no sense whatsoever! It would have seemed an absolute contradiction of their understanding of the nature of God.

Picture Joseph sitting alone in his carpenter shop, mulling it all over. Maybe the day is done and the red sun is drooping low over the Galilean skyline. Mary arrives, as is her custom, with a skin of water and a fresh-baked loaf, but he's so distant today. She picks up a palm branch and begins sweeping up his wood shavings from the afternoon's labor. There aren't as many shavings as there were two months ago. She notices, but says nothing.

He looks at her across the room. He wonders, "Did I hear God right? The whole town is laughing. They're taking their work to other craftsmen. She's so lovely. My father won't speak to me. My mother cries herself to sleep. Did I really hear God? Oh, God . . ."

But somehow he makes the right choice. He presses through, day by day. Against all odds, against all sense, against all opposition, he clings singularly to God's promise and as the days turn into months suddenly finds himself staring at the city gates of his ancestors—Bethlehem.

But somehow he makes the right choice.

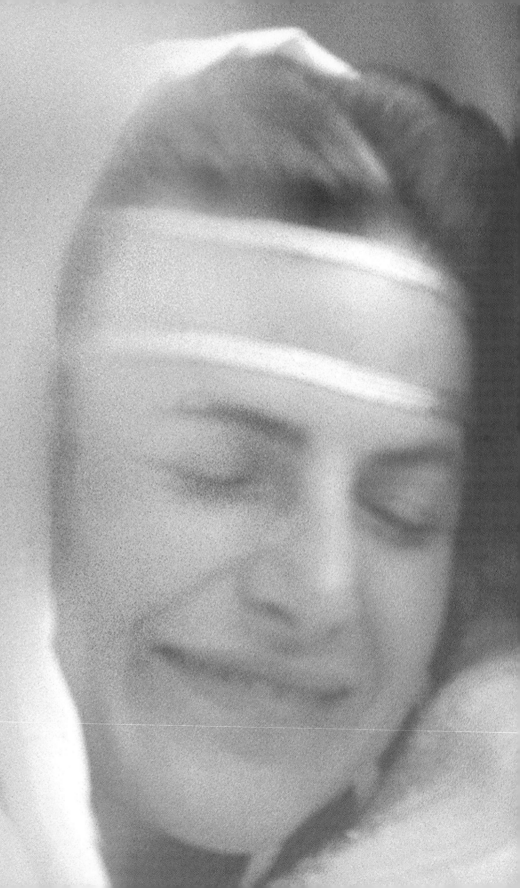

He took her

home as his wife.

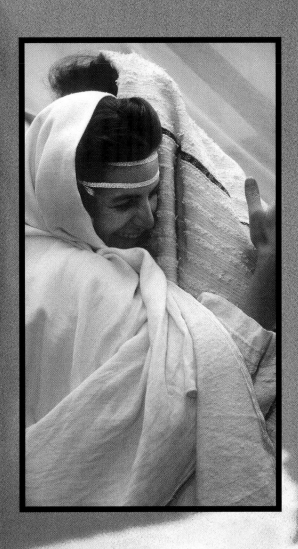

What a night that must have been for Joseph—his wife is going into labor, and he has no place for her to even rest, let alone give birth to her child. I would think a guy would want so much to provide for his wife, to take care of her and cover her with security and comfort. But here's this man, and no matter how hard he tries, there's no room anywhere and no money to convince an innkeeper to make room. There's not even any compassion for his wife and baby—just a city full of slammed doors.

Can you imagine the frustration, the sense of failure? Here he is, facing his first big challenge as a husband, and he can't even put a roof over his wife's head. Can you imagine the questions racing through his mind: "This isn't going right! Where are You, God? Why aren't You providing? I'm just trying to do what You've asked me to do! Why are You making it so hard?"

In a last-ditch effort, he manages a stable, possibly a cave. Can you imagine his shame, looking into his wife's eyes, seeing her pain and discomfort as she lies in the dirt and straw, engulfed in the smell of livestock?

And suddenly it's not just her—it's this baby—this baby boy whom he has been told to name "God saves"—Jesus—because He "will save His people from their sins." This baby of whom the prophet Isaiah had written centuries before that a virgin would be with child and give birth to a son, and call Him "God with us"—Immanuel. This baby of whom he and his wife had been told just months before: "He will be great and will be called the Son of the Most High. The Lord God will give Him the throne of His father David, and He will reign over the house of Jacob forever; His kingdom will never end." *Jesus.*

Birthed in a barn, a place animals are birthed. A dubious palace for One who will reign over the house of Jacob.

Laid in a trough from which animals eat. A dubious throne for one who will be called the Son of the Most High, whose kingdom will never end. A dubious throne for God-with-us.

This is Messiah—King of kings, Lord of lords! Where's the splash? Where's the thunder? Where are the flashing white lights and jeweled mansions? Where's the glory?

> This is My glory, My child: that I love you so much, I gave My Son—
> whom I love so much—to be made lower than the angels, to be made of no
> reputation, to be humbled, to be made nothing, *for you.*

> A barn. A peasant girl. A feed trough. A carpenter's son. *For you.*

> This is My glory, child. This is majesty. *Jesus!*

He was the Son of the

Living God, and His first

introduction to the humanity

He had come to serve was

murder, pride, fear, and

agony. And so His first steps

are taken, His first thoughts

are formed, His first words

are uttered as a refugee in the

shadow of Egypt's pagan gods.

Herod . . . gave orders to kill all the boys in Bethlehem and its vicinity . . .

Take the child and
His mother and escape to Egypt.

Joseph, Mary, and the child would spend the years following that most magnificently anonymous night running from a king's raging jealousy. Barely out of the womb, and already it had begun.

Herod . . . gave orders to kill all the boys in Bethlehem and its vicinity who were two years old and under.

Many mothers would cry in the streets as a result of those orders, their tears mixing in the dirt with the blood of their slaughtered babies.

Then what was said through the prophet Jeremiah was fulfilled:
"A voice is heard in Ramah, weeping and great mourning,
Rachel weeping for her children and refusing to be comforted,
because they are no more."

But eventually the jealous king would die, and the boy and his family would return to the friendly confines of the town His parents no doubt longed for and told stories of night after night. He would meet His cousins, His aunts and uncles, and when it came time for His king-training, He would not slip into a silken robe or take a golden scepter in His hand—no, that's not what this king or His kingdom was all about. Rather He would slip into a tattered and stained apron and take a hammer and chisel in hand.

The apron would be His royal robe, the hammer His scepter, and for the next 25 or more years, this insignificant little town, this carpenter shop, would be His royal court and kingdom.

And the child grew and became strong;
He was filled with wisdom, and the grace of God was upon Him.

"Sovereign Lord, as You have promised,
You now dismiss Your servant in peace.
For my eyes have seen Your salvation,
which You have prepared in the sight of all people,
a light for revelation to the Gentiles
and for glory to Your people Israel."

REPENT!
FOR THE KINGDOM

*On those living
in the land of
the shadow of death,
a light has dawned.*

OF HEAVEN IS NEAR!

chapter two

They were words that had been sitting on the edge of His lips, tickling and teasing His tongue for decades, words He'd dreamed of proclaiming from the mountaintops and street corners of ancient Israel night after restless night: "Repent, for the kingdom of heaven is near!"

Once, when He was only 12, He stepped out. He sat in the temple courts among the most learned of the learned, astounding them to silence with wisdom and understanding not only beyond His own tender years, but beyond all they themselves had gleaned from their four or five or more decades of devotion to the law and prophets.

Little did they realize at the time, but all of their study, all of their feasts, all of their fasting, prayer, and sacrifice would be captured in that simple proclamation, that bottom-line essence: "Repent! For the kingdom of heaven is near!"

But in spite of the 12-year-old's unearthly wisdom, it was not yet His time. There were years—no, decades—of shaping and trying, of testing and forging. There was a perfection of timing, a perfection of obedience, a specific millisecond that had been ordained since the foundations of the universe, that had to be waited upon, and waited upon, and then waited upon some more.

There was a process, a pattern, a plan established in the heavenlies thousands of years earlier, before the dust of the earth below His growingly calloused feet was formed into tangible substance. "Repent, for the kingdom of heaven is near!"

But suddenly He was there, kissing His mother goodbye, packing a modest satchel, walking away from every companionship and security He'd ever known, trekking over mountain high and valley low and exploding like a rocket of magnificence from the muddy waters of a Jordan baptism:

"It is proper for us to do this to fulfill all righteousness."

Finally, glory like we love glory! The very Spirit of God Himself descending like a dove! A voice splitting the heavens without reservation: "You are My Son whom I love; with You I am well pleased!" High beyond high! Excitement beyond excitement! Majesty beyond majesty!

At once, the Spirit sent Him out into the desert . . .

Cold, wind, sweat—and time. Time to think, time

to reflect, time to long for the sweet warmth of His

Nazareth yesterday and tremble at the ordained

horror of His Golgotha tomorrow.

Wind, sweat, time...

Wait, My Son.
This is what I have for You today.

Wait.

Forty days. It must have felt like 40 years. The pinnacle of His Holy Spirit baptism visitation, the laughter of distant family and friends, both ringing afresh in His heart, and suddenly there He is— alone. No food, no water, no shelter—alone. The same perfect will that spilled such glory upon Him yesterday now spills Him into the center of hell on earth today.

Cold, wind, sweat—and time. Time to think, time to reflect, time to long for the sweet warmth of His Nazareth yesterday and tremble at the ordained horror of His Golgotha tomorrow.

Time to hunger. Time to thirst. Time to shake against the frigid night and faint under the furnace day. Time to collapse at His Father's feet and cry out for something—anything—to eat, to drink, to shield, to protect, to give Him the strength to make it through the next day—no, the next hour, the next five minutes.

Oh, He could easily kick the ground beneath His feet and the sweetest spring of honey-water in all the universe would burst forth from the dry, cracked earth like a crystal fountain. He could easily take a stone in His blistered hand and with one thought transform it into the freshest of loaves, the choicest of meats. But . . . no. The Father says, "Wait, My Son. This is what I have for You today. Wait."

And so, against the scream of His every bodily cell and every human desire, He waits. He curls up at His Father's feet; He cries out for His Father's strength—and He waits. And when given the opportunity to satisfy Himself and deny the humanity that would spit in His face just a few short years later and for generations upon generations, He looks earthly goodness in the face and through the sand wedged between His teeth triumphantly belts, "Away from Me, Satan! For it is written: 'Worship the Lord Your God, and serve Him only.' "

It was then that the devil left Him. It was then that the angels attended Him. It was then that His Father smiled a smile that engulfed the very cosmos and magnificently whispered what He'd longed to whisper for centuries upon centuries: *"Now!"*

"Repent, for the kingdom of heaven is near!"

It's a message that ever-so-tragically carries the image of a crazed man on a street corner with a sandwich sign and megaphone. It's a message that is ever-so-misunderstood to speak of condemnation, judgment, Armageddon, and the wrath of almighty God.

But, praise God, nothing could be further from the truth. Repentance is not condemnation—it's liberation!

It's not judgment—it's joy! It's not Armageddon—it's new birth! It's not the crushing sneer of a wrathful God but an invitation to the party of parties, the excitement of excitements, the wedding banquet of wedding banquets—eternal life!

And it doesn't await some dark and ugly day of God's revenge, but "the kingdom of heaven is *near!*" It is now! It knocks at the door of your heart today and comes like a flood free for the asking!

I have to believe that when Jesus finally stood in some Galilean marketplace to unleash His streams of living water upon the world, He rose triumphantly to His feet, smiled a smile that would shame the sun, wiped the sweat free from His forehead, and exploded with all the holiness, joy, and majesty of the Man He unquestionably was—the Son of the Living God. "Repent, for the kingdom of heaven is near!" Translation: "Come and join the fun! Be free of all your sin! You don't have to live like you do for one more hour!"

Oh, what a marvelously magnificent day it must have been. And oh, what a shockingly ordinary day it must have been. I can't help but think of the people who shook their heads in disgust and walked past His invitation that morning. I can't help but think of the people who laughed to themselves and thought, "Here comes another one." And I can't help but think of Jesus at the campfire that night, tears in His eyes for His children so lost, so busy, so blindly and painfully burdened. He pulls His cloak up over His shoulder and lies down to sleep, accompanied only by a chorus of first-century crickets. His eyes open to gaze up at the wondrous heavens above, the star-speckled night sky that He and He alone knows was hand-hewn by His own design. *Jesus.*

Come morning, He would rise before dawn, make His way into town, and do it all again. He would stand in the same marketplace or sit in the same synagogue and speak the same invitation to the same people. He would not give up. No, He had been through so much already, and whether His heartcry would be heard by one or by hundreds of thousands, whether He would return to that campfire alone again or surrounded by multitudes, He was born for this very reason—for that one person—and He would rise to do it again, and again, and again—for that one:

He was born for this very reason—

for that one person.

"Repent, for the kingdom of heaven is near!"

· · · —————— ◎ —————— · · ·

Well, eventually, one of those mornings, someone, somehow, heard those words in the depth of his or her heart and stopped. Maybe it was someone rushing to work in the fields or a child sitting next to dad in a donkey cart. Maybe it was a woman whose husband had just handed her a certificate of divorce or a crippled beggar lying helplessly in a puddle of street garbage.

Something tells me it was the latter—someone so utterly desperate, so terribly broken. Someone with nothing of this world to lean on, nothing to be proud of or claim as his own. Some devastated somebody who knew only one thing: "My life's a mess, and I need God."

It's always those kinds of people, isn't it? People whose hearts have been chafed raw, people who have been exhausted of earthly resource, stripped to dry bone, rejected and spit out by the things they trusted and a world that welcomes only the beautiful and successful.

But whoever it was, the day came, the heart opened, and the floodwaters of God's grace began to breathe new life into hungry souls across the land. And before long, Jesus would look around His once lonely campfire and see a ragtag team of unlikely faces lounging about, listening, questioning, doubting, wondering. A thief, a prostitute, a couple of fishermen. A man who would sit beneath His cross and watch Him die, and a man who would sell Him into that death for pocket change.

Though thousands would eventually come, these few would be his closest. John, Peter, Mary Magdalene, Nathanael, Andrew, Philip. . . a questionable gathering of absolute nobodies who, for reasons probably beyond their own grasp, had each turned their backs and walked away from every security they had built in life and every heart's desire that had filled their every dream. Little did they realize that seemingly mindless decision—that decision their relatives and friends undoubtedly laughed at and scolded them for—would springboard them into the most remarkable, most privileged, most rare and extraordinary adventure in all of human experience: a day-by-day, side-by-side walk with the Son of the Living God.

Come . . . follow.

Can you imagine it? Eavesdropping on the deepest secrets of the kingdom of heaven. Eyewitnessing wisdom and wonders inconceivable to the furthest stretches of human imagination. Partaking in the most significant events of all time—events ordained since before the beginning and chosen to be the vehicle by which the doors of relationship with Father God Himself would be unlatched and flung open forever and for all.

It would be their daily lot. For the next two, maybe three, years, they would travel through the towns and villages, over the hillsides and valleys of their tiny country, tasting what prophets and righteous men had longed to taste for hundreds and hundreds of years—*Jesus.*

They would sit at Jesus' feet in Jerusalem's temple courts and sleep at His shoulder in Judea's wilderness. They would share meals with Him on the shore of Lake Galilee and shed tears alongside Him in the streets of Bethsaida. They would gaze into His eyes, hang on the tenor of His voice, dance to the joy-song of His salvation, and watch Him single-handedly alter the course of universal history—forever and always, to eternity.

> *Land of Zebulun and land of Naphtali,*
> *the way to the sea,*
> *along the Jordan,*
> *Galilee of the Gentiles—*
> *The people living in darkness have seen a great light;*
> *on those living in the land of the shadow of death,*
> *a light has dawned.*

Land of Zebulun and land of Naphtali,

the way to the sea,

along the Jordan,

Galilee of the Gentiles—

The people living in darkness have seen a great light;

on those living in the land of the shadow of death,

a light has dawned.

THIS IS MY SON, IN

What kind of man is this? Even the winds and the waves

WHOM I AM WELL PLEASED

obey Him!

chapter three

Three

How does one describe One who is utterly indescribable? How does one describe Jesus?

Hundreds of years before His infant cries first pierced the air of a Bethlehem stable, the city's most celebrated forefather, David, puts a prophetic pen to parchment—

> *You are the most excellent of men, and*
> *Your lips have been anointed with grace . . . .*

> *Gird Your sword upon Your side,*
> *O Mighty One . . . .*

> *In Your majesty ride forth victoriously in behalf*
> *of truth, humility, and righteousness . . . .*

> *Therefore God, Your God, has set You above Your*
> *companions by anointing You with the oil of joy.*

Beneath his celebration of words, you can't help but sense what had to have been King David's overwhelming frustration—the awareness that as hard as he's tried, he hasn't even begun to approach the object of his poetry with so much as a whisper of justice. The totality, the immensity, the intensity, the intimacy—the absolute wonder of what the Holy Spirit has breathed into his understanding barely lifts its head against the constraint of human vocabulary.

Jesus: the "most excellent of men"; "riding forth on behalf of truth, humility, and righteousness"; "anointed with grace; anointed with joy."

Can you imagine the absolutely explosive human being He must have been? Think of His reality— here He is, walking among His creation, feeling between His divine toes the crackle and crunch of the earth His own hands formed in centuries past. He stands waist-deep in the Sea of Galilee. The wind He calls by name whips through the tangles of His own hair; the waves He set in motion slap against His bare chest.

Jesus

You are the most excellent of men.

Therefore God, Your God, has set

You above Your companions by

anointing You with the oil of joy.

I picture Him on the Mount of Olives as day breaks, exploding in wonder and dancing in praise to His Father at the grandeur of His own sun rising across the Judean horizon, celebrating the magnificence that He alone is aware of.

He alone could understand the vastness of what His life would count for. His every step, every encounter, had been ordained from the beginning of time—every smile and every tear. His every conversation and relationship a pressing forward into the excitement of excitements: the salvation of His children and the indescribably miraculous triumph that that is.

Folklore and formality have done a good job of painting Jesus slight and solemn, distant and detached, of reducing Him to a long-faced, stained-glass image. But this was God in the flesh! This was all the bigness and power, the goodness and glory, the might and the majesty of the universe and then some, somehow incredibly wrapped up in the confines of a human body.

His were hands that had flung the stars into the sky, lips that had kissed the moon into being. He stood before the people and joyously proclaimed, "Before Abraham was born, I am!"

And now, here He is, living earthly life in earthly time. Walking among and living with the throngs of His most treasured, most valued, most beloved creation: *people*. Laughing with them, eating with them, working with them, crying over them. On a mission of redemptive love—the liberating of their lives into the salvation of their souls.

He alone knows the value of those souls, the value of their lives. He alone knows the priority that they are—such priority that the Son of the Living God gladly leaps from heavenly perfection and dives headlong into hellish destruction to save even one of them from the same fate.

He presses in with tireless fervor, marching forward with the confident stride of a man who knows what His life is all about, never once indulging a disappointment, never once wasting an opportunity, never once holding a regret or complaint or looking back. Just pressing in and pressing on, "riding forth victoriously" from town to town and life to life, bringing joy and healing, truth and liberty! And all for that one who would stop and be saved.

His were hands that had flung the stars into the sky.

Can you imagine what it must have been like for the people 2000 years ago? To look into His eyes, to hear the belt of His voice, to feel the touch of His hand?

It would not have been a soft hand, you know. It would have been an experienced, calloused, thick-with-muscle hand. It would have been a hand that radiated strength, protection, bigness, tenderness.

It would have been a hand whose every touch was pure and giving, a hand that lifted, a hand that covered, a hand that cherished, a hand you just knew you could trust—and that whispered with its every touch, "I love you. I love you. I love you."

And then there was His voice. It would not necessarily have been the booming Shakespearean baritone of religious myth. He was God, and He most certainly would not have sought to establish His authority through such shallow attractions.

No, it was not tonal quality or oratory presence that gripped the people 2000 years ago, but passion . . . *urgency*.

You see, He alone knows the fullness of life that His Father promises, and the vastness of death in life that flows from simple lack of trusting Him. He alone sees the loneliness and brokenness behind the laughter and bravado, the self-destruction beneath the masks of "righteousness."

It floods through His physical, emotional, and spiritual senses like a tidal wave. It is His constant awareness—and so His heart breaks. It breaks into a million pieces, and His voice erupts in a volcano of compassion, pouring forth eternity-altering, uncontestable truth in a depth of heartcry that begs the people with every syllable of every word of every teaching and every parable, "Come to Me! Learn from Me! I'm gentle—I'm humble in heart! You'll find rest for your soul."

Hands that whispered with

every touch, "I love you.

I love you. I love you."

Strength

For theirs is the kingdom of heaven.

And then He turns, and from all the way across the marketplace or hillside, His welcoming eyes meet yours and silently breathe, "I know you. Mine are the hands that created you. They formed you while you were yet in your mother's womb—and I know you."

Yes, this truly was "the most excellent of men," and there would be little doubt the very second you laid eyes on Him. Explosively joyous, explosively alive, robust, hands-on, bigger-than-life, and as down-to-earth as it gets. The living definition of a hero.

It is astounding to consider—here was the Son of God, with all the power of heaven and earth and beyond at His fingertips, and what He chose to do with 100 percent of it, 100 percent of the time, was to give it away! Giving, giving, and then giving some more would be the core, the fountainhead, of all that He was and did—the source of His joy and the life-breath of His excellence.

It's true! As the Gospel records, Jesus never once used even the tiniest measure of His vastness of resource for Himself. It was always for other people. It was always to the honor of His Father and for the well-being of other people.

Think of it: He gives sight to a man blind from birth—He sleeps in the dirt, shivering against a camp-fire's embers. He feeds hungry thousands with a prayer of thanks—He sends His disciples into town to buy something to eat. He raises a little girl from the dead—He lays quietly on a piece of wood while a common man drives nails through His hands and feet.

Can you even begin to imagine the glory and excitement that bubbles within and flows out of a man like that? Free in His heart to give without inhibition or reserve! Can you even begin to fathom the love for people—love the apostle Paul terms "the most excellent way"—from which such choices cascade and cascade and cascade again?

It was always to the honor of His Father and for the well-being of other people.

The softness of every sunrise.
The promise of every rainbow.

Go back and report . . . what you hear and see:
The blind receive sight, the lame walk, those who have leprosy are cured,
the deaf hear, the dead are raised, and the good news is preached to the poor.

Jesus, Jesus, Jesus—
Jesus just being Jesus.

How does one describe One who is utterly indescribable? Is there a word that means joy but is beyond incomprehensible joy? A word that encompasses the thunder of every waterfall, the dance of every brook, the laughter of every baby in the nestle of every daddy's arms?

Is there a word that means passion? A word that gathers the roar of every lion, the blast of every volcano, the peal and crash of every wave that ever exploded against a seashore?

Is there a word that means intimacy and warmth? A word that bottles the softness of every sunrise, the promise of every rainbow, the twinkle of every star, the tiptoe of every doe and fawn between every forest's autumn leaves?

Is there a word that means love? A word that means kindness? A word that means power, bigness, humility, purity?

I know of only one such word. It is the most awe-inspiring, breath-stealing, unequivocally magnificent word in this language or any other. Ironically it is a mere five letters, yet it carries a truth and meaning so big, so life-changing, so nation- and eternity-altering if only given the chance.

It is the word of words. The single word that every human life right along with its every human hope and struggle is answered by and resolved in. It is the beginning, and it is the end. It is the fullness of life, the gateway to eternity, the hope of the ages. It is . . .

Jesus

It is the word of words. The single word that every

human life right along with its every human hope

and struggle is answered by and resolved in. It is the

beginning, and it is the end. It is the fullness of life,

the gateway to eternity, the hope of the ages.

COME

To bind up the broken hearted . . .

To comfort all who mourn . . .

To bestow on them a crown of beauty

instead of ashes, the oil of gladness

instead of mourning

and a garment of praise

instead of a spirit of despair.

TO ME!

chapter four

Four

Have you never read,
"From the lips of children and infants You have ordained praise"?

They came to Jesus as children 2000 years ago; made children by their diseases, their blindnesses, their poverties; by their twisted bodies, their desperate hearts, their empty purses, their hungry spirits. They came as children, and He healed them.

It is a startling truth, crying out for its due from the pages of Scripture, crying over its abandonment by man. So quickly and so tragically we trade in our dirty knees and scraped elbows for combed hair and clean fingernails. Our tears before God become a suit coat and a study guide in the name of "spiritual maturity."

But the living Word of God as trumpeted from the lungs of the Son of the Living God is very clear in its cry: *This is what spiritual maturity is—*

> *Whoever humbles himself like this child*
> *is the greatest in the kingdom of heaven.*

> *Unless you change and become like little children,*
> *you will never enter the kingdom of heaven.*

And so, 2000 years ago, grasping that truth in the gut of her desperation, a grown woman crawls through the dirt, chasing the hem of a stranger's robe. A soldier kneels before the same stranger on behalf of a dying child. A thief scampers into the branches of a fig tree to catch a glimpse of Him passing by. A prostitute bathes His feet in the tears of her brokenness. A man blind from birth dances before the religious authority. A woman calls herself a dog as she pleads for an end to her daughter's pain. And all the host of heavenly glory leap for joy as their precious Lamb-upon-the-Throne dances on that throne and exclaims, "Yes! 'For the kingdom of heaven belongs to such as these.' "

Whoever humbles himself like this child

is the greatest in the kingdom of heaven.

One of the dangers of our familiarity with the events of Jesus' life and interactions is a jading to the raw realities of what really happened out there 2000 years ago, and who really was involved. As wonderful as all of the sermons and studies, the hymns and top-40 hits, the church plays and theological analyses are, in the quest for higher truth what very well could be the highest truth of all gets driven over: These were *real people* 2000 years ago. These were not caricatures or symbols or devices manipulated by God to teach future generations, but very real, very-much-like-you-and-me people.

The paralytic man whom Jesus healed 2000 years ago was not then "The Paralytic Man." He was a *man*—living, breathing, not unlike any man reading this page; full of hope for his life, dreams of a wife and family, and a thriving career at whatever trade or talent bubbled in his heart.

Assuming his body was not bent from birth, I think of him as a boy, perhaps sitting on the shore of Galilee watching the fishing boats come in as the sun limps low in the horizon, hearing the men sing and shout of their catches across each other's bow. "I want to fish," he whispers to himself. "I want to live my life on the sea. I want to be like them."

Or maybe he's walking hand-in-hand with his mother through the marketplace, spying the rare linens and exotic spices and seeing the finely adorned camels on whose backs goods were carried from distant lands. "I want to be a merchant." The boy's imagination soars. "I want to travel and taste the farthest kingdoms of the world."

And then comes the day when the boy's limbs dry and wither, his dreams along with them. I don't know what it was—an accident perhaps, a disease maybe—but his legs seized and turned to stone. They gave way to numbness, and with it went any hope in his first-century world of ever making a living, let alone feeling the sea-salt spray in his face or the far east wind skipping through the curls of his hair.

And so, in the imprisonment of a functionless body, his ambitions change. As he lies on his mat day after day, month and year after month and year, he dreams no longer of a prize-winning catch of fish but of his right hand somehow clutching a single chunk of fish, somehow lifting it to his mouth. Yes, his life's ambition has become to someday, some way, feed himself with his own hand.

He stares at the wall opposite him, and his imagination drifts not to lands far away but to the six steps it would take to cross the room and touch that wall. The tears he's shed night after night, thinking about that wall. Oh, what he'd give to just once touch that wall.

There are times when life gets reduced to its most basic. There are times when our fanciful pursuits, our grand visions, and our sophistication explode in a puff of reality and we are faced, like that man, with wanting just one step, one hour without pain, one hand to hold, one piece of bread, one more breath to stay alive for one more second.

And so, like a child, the man begs anyone close enough to see the desperation in his tears, "Take me to Jesus."

Sweet desperation. The fervent prayer of a righteous man.

"Lord, help me!"
"Lord! Have mercy on my son!"
"If only I touch His cloak."

Yes, it was in their desperation that Jesus met the people. For it is in that place where the sophisticate becomes a fool, the scholar becomes a student, the tough becomes tender, the elegant plead and beg, and the much-too-grown-up throws all of his polish and togetherness away for the simple heart *of a child*.

And standing among them, erupting in joy, Jesus thrusts His arms toward the heavens above and belts from the deepest recesses of His more-than-obvious divinity:

> *"I praise You, Father, Lord of heaven and earth,*
> *because You have hidden these things from the wise and learned,*
> *and revealed them to little children.*
> *Yes, Father, for this was Your good pleasure."*

Then He turns a sun-shaming smile to the paralytic man and everyone like him from 2000 years ago to today and tomorrow's tomorrow. He lifts the face, He wipes the tear, He looks deep into the eyes and breathes His peace:

> Take heart, daughter; take heart, son.
> Be freed from your suffering.
> *Your sins are forgiven!*

Yes, they came to Him in their pain; crawling through the dirt, lying on a mat, begging in the street; torn, rejected, used, afraid—they came, *and He healed them.*

He reached a thick, gentle, divine hand right into their wounds. He threw a warm, strong, divine embrace around their naked shoulders. He wept a thousand compassionate, divine tears over their broken lives—*and He healed them.*

Can you imagine? He stops, turns from the crowd, and looks right into your eyes—the Son of the Living God. It's as if your heart and your history lie bare before Him. The speech you'd prepared and rehearsed suddenly gets swallowed beneath the tidal wave of acceptance that spills from His gaze, and your lips mumble words so simple, so unsophisticated, so gloriously childlike: "Lord, if You are willing, You can make me clean."

Your face drops in shame at the sound of them; tears leak from your eyes. *What could I possibly have been thinking? He's the Son of God—what could I possibly mean to Him?*

And immediately crushing that lie of lies, a voice—tender and quivering in tears of its own, in heartbreak over your heartbreak—unequivocally responds with the impossible, "I am willing. Be clean."

I am willing...

His love that compels Him to reach into your wounds and cry

for your loss and muster all the power of the universe to restore

what was destroyed, redeem what was squandered, resurrect

what was presumed dead. It is His love—His love for you.

It's *His* voice! Oh, yes! And it's *His* body that moves toward you and drops into the dirt beside you; *His* hand that reaches out and actually touches you; *His* love that explodes through your spirit, soul, and body, squalling up like a mighty wind and blasting away every tatter and tear, every compromise and confusion, every rejection and rebellion from yesterday and today to beyond the beyond. Glory to the Living God!

Yes, it is His love that makes Him stop everything He's doing; His love that makes Him turn all of His attention on you; His love that compels Him to reach into your wounds and cry for your loss and muster all the power of the universe to restore what was destroyed, redeem what was squandered, resurrect what was presumed dead. It is His love—His love for *you.*

And in the ecstasy of celebration that follows, far beyond the flesh that's miraculously pulsating with new life, far beyond the heart that's beating with new joy, is a bigger, more astounding thing—a life-altering revelation—that sets your feet to dancing and causes you to leap into His embrace and collapse into His arms and weep like a baby . . .

He loves me.
He's the Son of the Living God,
and He loves me.

It is true, my child. And there is nothing you can do to change that.
I do love you—pure and simple.
I am God—
I gave My life for you; My life is for you;
and I love you.
Jesus

It is the mystery of mysteries, the reality of realities. It is the one constant, the solution to it all, clawing for air beneath the mudslide of human foolishness and self-seeking. It is the most precious, most maligned, most longed for, most fundamental, most pushed away, most sought after, most mistrusted, most cherished mystery/reality in all of human history: He is the Son of the Living God, and what He chooses to do with it is love *you.*

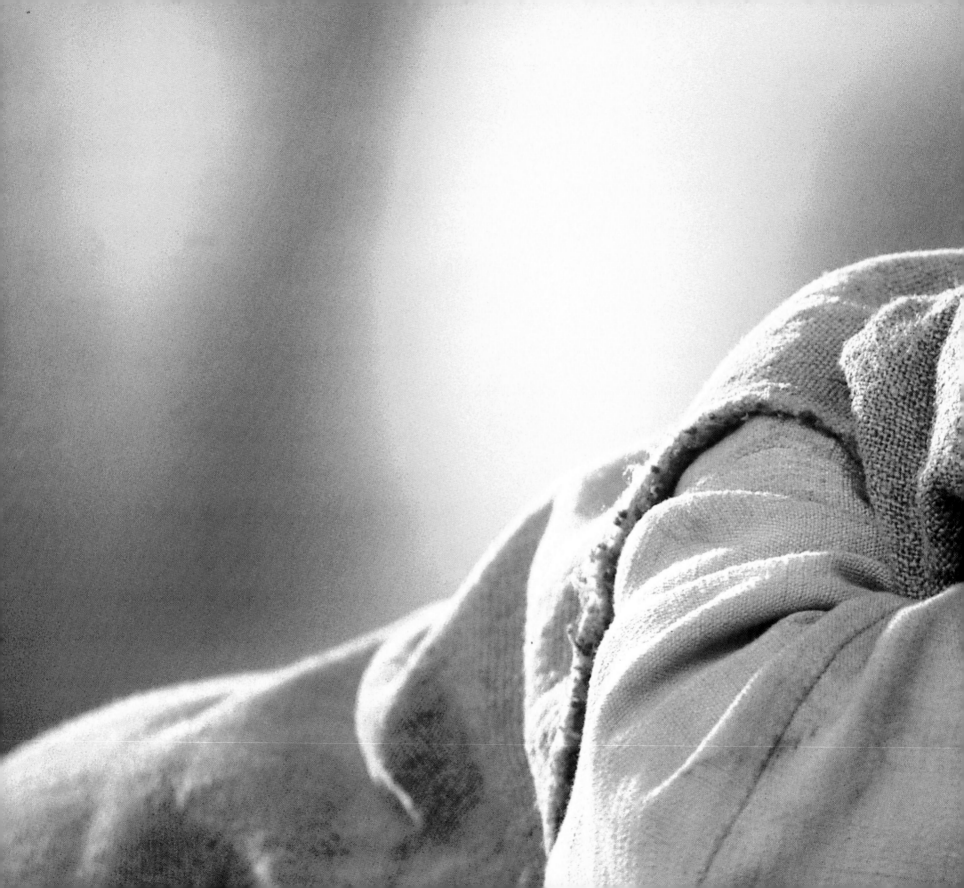

Whether it's giving His life in hanging from a tree or giving His life in the streets and marketplaces of ancient Judea, it's all the same thing: He loves you.

Whether it's bleeding from the wounds of three Roman spikes, or bleeding from the wounds of a heart pierced with compassion, it's all the same thing: He loves you.

He loves you, He loves you, He loves you.
Jesus.

There were many who were blind 2000 years ago; many who were crippled; many whose sons and daughters and fathers and brothers were demon-possessed or dead or languishing neck-deep in pits of the worst kind of poverty yet would choose that blindness, that lameness, that death rather than bend a single knee or shed a single tear in His presence.

You see, there is a blindness far worse than not being able to see. There is a paralysis far worse than legs that are bent and twisted. There is a death far beyond the tomb, a demon-possession far beyond fits of lunacy, a poverty far more devastating than starvation.

It is a disease that Jesus longed to heal and liberate His children from more than any other 2000 years ago, more than any other today. It is the filth of filths, the hell of hells. It is pride, self-righteousness, self-justification, self-pursuit, self-reliance.

And so, one priest calls Him a devil; another calls Him a bastard. A lawyer meets His offer of love with riddles. A wealthy man walks away. And the religious esteemed drag a helpless girl through the temple courts with rocks in their hands and murder in their hearts.

From that time on
Jesus began to explain to His disciples
that He must go to Jerusalem and suffer many things . . .

"O JERUSALEM,

How often I have longed

to gather

your children together,

as a hen gathers her chicks

under her wings . . .

JERUSALEM..."

chapter five

He loved them as well, you know—the Pharisees, the Saducees, the religious authorities and teachers of the law.

Many attacked Him. They challenged Him, mocked Him, lied about him, plotted against Him, and did all they could to destroy Him. And in our 2000-years-later-hindsight, how we hate them for it.

But not Jesus. On the day, in the heat of the battle, with the spit dripping down His face and their laughter ringing in His ears, with the clothes being torn from His back and the whip slicing across His flesh, *oh, how He loved them* in the midst of it.

It's an astounding truth—so astounding, some would deny it.

But He is "no respecter of persons"; there is "none righteous, no, not one"; and He came to "seek and save what was lost," not push them away. And in that, as mind-bending as it may seem, the cry of His heart was exactly the same to the religious leaders—the men He knew would rejoice in the streets at the smell of His blood mixing with sand—as to anyone else: "Come to Me . . . and you will find rest for your souls."

When we think of Jesus coming to seek and save "the lost," we tend to envision drug addicts, prostitutes, convicts, and the like. But on a closer look, who could possibly be more lost than one who assumes, by virtue of his own righteousness, his own education, perhaps his own superior lifestyle, that he doesn't need to be found? Oh, the heartbreak of such lostness! Lostness beyond lostness.

And so these men, appointed, entrusted, by Father God to bless and shepherd His children, adorn themselves from head to toe in flamboyant displays of presumed holiness, strutting among the people like heaven's own peacocks, sitting proudly in the front-row seats of first-century Israel, pontificating and dissertating on what they thought was the law with such jot-and-tittle precision that they missed "The Law" completely, though they longed, probably more than anyone else, to look into His eyes and lay their crowns at His feet.

"I have shown

you many great

miracles . . . .

For which of

these do you

stone Me?"

He would beg them
to open their hearts.

Well, they did look into His eyes. In fact, at 12 years old, slipping away from His father and mother and into the temple courts of Jerusalem, Jesus chose to go to them first. Some 20 years later, slipping away from Judea and into the synagogues of Galilee, He again went to them first.

And He would keep going to them. He would continue to reveal Himself to them. He would beg them to open their hearts. He would weep when they turned their backs. He would push the grief from His soul, pray for them from the depth of His compassion, wipe the exhaustion from His eyes, and go to them— again, and again, and again.

"I have shown you many great miracles from the Father.
For which of these do you stone Me?"

Yes, they would look into His eyes, day after day, month after month, for two, perhaps three, years. And what they would see in His every glance was His love for them, His heartbreak over them, His conviction of them.

And one day, on a hill named Golgotha, after all was said and done, they would get the chance to lay those crowns at His feet. They wouldn't be the crowns of gold they'd anticipated for generations upon generations, but then He wasn't the king they'd anticipated either.

It is a great mystery. If anyone should have recognized that Jesus was Messiah, it was these very men—the Pharisees and teachers of the law—who fought Him tooth and nail, and stood as His enemy every step of the way.

You see, they studied the Scriptures like no one else. They knew the messianic prophecies of old like no one else. They could quote it all backward and forward, inside out and upside down. They lived it and breathed it and begged Father God for it every day of their lives.

See, your king comes to you, gentle and riding on a donkey.

He had no beauty or majesty . . .
He will not judge by what He sees with His eyes . . .
but with righteousness He will judge the needy,
with justice He will give decisions for the poor.

The spirit of the Lord will rest on Him.

Righteousness will be His belt
and faithfulness the sash around His waist.

Behold your king comes to you,

Hosanna

gentle and riding on a donkey . . .

So there He was riding a donkey, the people hailing Him as king—and they missed it. There He was, sleeves rolled up, sporting nothing of human flash—and they missed it. There He was, in the dirt with the poor and needy—and they missed it. There He was, exploding with the Spirit of God—opening the eyes of the blind, lifting the dead from their graves, begging them with tears and confrontation to turn from their petty displays, to dive to their knees and from the bottom of their hearts crave *authentic* righteousness, *kingdom* faithfulness, and praise that comes from God, not men.

> *"Blind Pharisee!*
> *First clean the inside of the cup and dish,*
> *and then the outside also will be clean."*

But they missed it. Heartbreak of heartbreaks, they opted for stubborn pride despite the obvious, and missed it, and missed it, and kept right on missing it.

For with all of His true and evident magnificence—magnificence *of the heart*—Jesus just wasn't who they wanted Him to be. They wanted pageantry and splendor, worldly riches, earthly thrones, politics, rules, regulations.

In other words, they wanted Him to be like they were, and the fact that He wasn't—the fact that He was more interested in people than pomp, in goodness than glory; more interested in salvation than Sabbath, righteousness than rightness—was undoubtedly the greatest offense of all.

Despite who they thought Messiah would be, what stood in front of them was who Messiah *was*. What stood in front of them was simple love—love beyond love—feeding a hungry person, healing a broken life, resurrecting a tortured spirit. What stood in front of them was Jesus.

> *"If any of you has a sheep and it falls into a pit on the Sabbath,*
> *will you not . . . lift it out?*
> *How much more valuable is a man than a sheep?"*

Oh, a few of them would acknowledge His truth. A few would have their hearts pierced through the concrete layers of false expectation. One would even slip out beneath the cover of night and seek His counsel. Others would tiptoe from shadow to shadow and whisper to no one's ear, "Surely, this man is The Prophet."

But such utterance would easily give way to fear of man and be drowned in the deluge of self-accommodating folly: "This fellow is blaspheming!" "By the prince of demons . . . He drives out demons!"

And so their only salvation—the answer to all their prayers and their forefathers' prayers—collapses in the temple courts under the weight of having done everything He possibly could and sobs for the lostness of their souls.

Oh, what a day that must have been. With the sun barely breaching the city walls, the Savior enters Jerusalem, knowing the showdown that would take place, knowing the futility His passions would fall on and the cross they would lead Him to in but a few short days.

O Jerusalem, Jerusalem,

you who kill the prophets and stone those sent to you,

how often I have longed to gather your children together,

as a hen gathers her chicks under her wings . . .

For I tell you,

"Blessed is He who comes in the

you will not see Me again until you say,

name of the Lord."

"Woe to you, teachers of the law and Pharisees, you hypocrites! . . .
How will you escape being condemned to hell? . . .
For I tell you, you will not see Me again until you say,
'Blessed is He who comes in the name of the Lord.' "

It was His last-ditch effort. From day one, He had answered their every challenge, their every question. He had reasoned with them, explained Himself to them, loved them, invited them, rebuked them. He had displayed all the wonders of His Father's glory in front of their eyes time and time again. He'd pled with them to know Him and to know His Father, time and time again.

But the Passover that would end all Passovers was a mere two days away. The clock had all but run out. Within 48 hours, those whose souls He'd just wept for would assemble and plot their final arrangements, thrusting Him into fulfillment of the very prophecies they denied He was the fulfillment of.

"But not during the Feast . . . or there may be a riot among the people."

One of His closest companions would assist them in those "arrangements."

"What are you willing to give me if I hand Him over to you?"

One of His dearest friends would swear on oath that he never knew Him.

"Before the rooster crows, you will disown Me three times."

The thousands who'd praised Him just the day before would scream for His murder.

"Let His blood be on us and on our children!"

And being the Lamb bred to be slaughtered, He would hang between heaven and earth and perform His greatest miracle ever.

"The hour has come. Look, the Son of Man is betrayed into the hands of sinners.

Rise! Let us go! Here comes My betrayer!"

Before the rooster crows you will

disown Me three times . . .

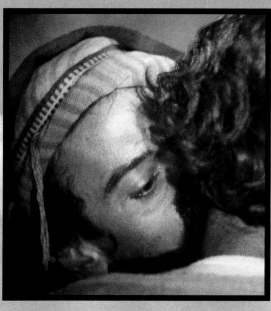

One of you will betray Me . . .

HE IS WORTHY

*Greater love
has no one than this,
that he lay down his life...*

"He is worthy of death."

It was a simple, straightforward declaration, unmistakable in its intent. Five words, six syllables, 17 letters, given voice in the black of night as Jesus stood before the religious authority bound by chains He could have turned to powder with but a thought.

It was a declaration so incredibly, so blatantly, so obviously wrong—the fact that it was ever uttered is as astounding as Lazarus stepping out of his grave.

I often think of the man who dared to speak it. Undoubtedly, there had been times when he had wandered into the marketplace or sat in the synagogue, listening, watching. Undoubtedly, he'd seen Jesus in the dirt weeping tears for people's pain and recognized in the hope of his heart, *This has to be the Way.* Undoubtedly he'd heard Jesus speak words from the throne room of heaven itself and sensed in the pit of his gut, *This has to be the Truth.* Undoubtedly, he'd witnessed Jesus giving sight to dead eyes and breath to dead bones, and known in the very depth of his creation, *This Man has to be the Life!*

But unfathomably, in the face of all that and more, the words still leak from His mortally mistaken lips: "He is worthy of death." The words leak, and the horror begins.

> *Many bulls surround Me;*
> *strong bulls of Bashan encircle Me.*
> *They hurl insults, shaking their heads.*
>
> *The Lord looks down from heaven on the sons of men*
> *to see if there are any who understand, any who seek God.*
>
> *"But I am a worm and not a man."*
>
> *"Dogs have surrounded Me;*
> *a band of evil men has encircled Me,*
> *they have pierced My hands and My feet."*

"I am poured out like water. . ."

"My bones are all out of joint. . ."

"My tongue sticks to the roof of My mouth. . ."

"My strength is dried up. . ."

"My heart has turned to wax. . ."

"My God, My God, why have You forsaken Me?"

———————

Blow by blow, lash by lash, lie by lie, nail by nail. Horror to end all horrors.

The spit flew, the hammer fell, the blood flowed

—and you and I were born again.

"What shall I say?

'Father, save Me from

this hour'?

No, it was for this

very reason

I came to this hour."

I am poured out like water . . .

*And when Jesus had cried out
again in a loud voice,*

He gave up His spirit.

There are so many things I could try to say here; adjectives, superlatives, graphic narrations and analogies I could try to draw in an attempt to somehow convey even a tiny sense of the realities Jesus swallowed that day 2000 years ago. The trauma, the terror, the pain—voluminous, incomprehensible pain.

It would be openly criminal for any one of us ever to minimize it or filter it through rose-colored glasses. Worse yet—tragedy of tragedies—to mock it, reject it, or, God forbid, shrug a casual shoulder at it.

My heart quakes to think of the passerby who looked up into what was left of His face that day and flippantly jested, "He trusts in the Lord; let the Lord rescue him." History has recorded how Jesus looked down from the cross and spoke, "They do not know what they are doing." In the case of this fellow, he knew not what he was saying. Oh, how awful the day when it was revealed to him. My heart also quakes for the passerby who would look into Jesus' face today and respond as carelessly, "Not interested." For God so loved the world that He gave His Son, that whoever would believe in Him would not perish but have eternal life.

You see, there is the religion of the cross, the intellectualization of the cross, the glamorization of the cross, and even—it kills me to write the words—the debate over the cross. But clawing for air beneath the avalanche of all that and more is the reality—the *truth*—of the cross.

And that truth is this: Jesus—the Son of the Living God—a Man possessing all the power and ability in the universe to stop the horror any time He wanted—chose not to consider Himself but to allow common men to tear the clothes off His back, spit in His face, drive nails through His limbs, and hang Him up to die in the afternoon sun.

And in the middle of it all, with a steady flow of blood twisting across His body and dripping off His toes into the sand beneath His feet, Jesus speaks words unfathomable, words eternal to those who looked on with their eyes that day and to us who look on with our hearts this day:

"Father, forgive them . . ."

You see, there is a way that seems right to a man—to take for oneself; to gather to oneself; to provide for, secure, and save oneself. And then there is the better way, the Jesus way, the way He chose to live every day of His life and every moment of His death: to give without regard for oneself; to provide for, secure, and ultimately, heroically, triumphantly, magnificently, save others—*at the cost of oneself.*

Why? Why would the Son of the Living God, who, if anyone deserved royal treatment in this life it was He, choose a path like that?

As the prophet Isaiah wrote centuries before a nondescript carpenter and his pregnant wife loaded up their donkey and journeyed toward Bethlehem, "He took up *our* infirmities . . . carried *our* sorrows . . . was pierced for *our* transgressions . . . was crushed for *our* iniquities."

In other words,

because He loves you.

Not long ago I was reading chapter 12 of the Bible's book of Hebrews where it says, "For the joy set before Him, Jesus endured the cross." I'd read those words many times, but for some reason this particular day, it really caught me. I leaned back in my chair and thought, *What joy? What joy could there possibly have been in an awful, hell-ridden thing like that?*

I prayed and prayed, and after the longest time, words rose in my heart; words for me, words for you, words for everyone reading this page and beyond, for He has the same heart, the same hope, the same desire and passion for everyone and for all.

> **The joy set before Me was you.**
> **You are My joy.**
> **That the day would come when we would share sweet companionship,**
> **today, tomorrow, and for all eternity.**
> **It is you, My beloved.**
> *It is you.*

Jesus

Father, forgive them . . .

AND

Why do you look for the living among the dead?

YET HE LIVES!

chapter seven

"Why do you look for the living among the dead?"

His story would not end on that ugly mound outside Jerusalem's wall that day. Quite the contrary, little did any among those who looked on—those who laughed or those who cried—even begin to suspect what was so humanly unsuspectable, so divinely foregone: *It was only just beginning!*

Not that He hadn't made it completely clear to them. Every warning He ever spoke of the upcoming Golgotha was punctuated with the remarkable and mysterious exclamation, *"But after three days . . . !"*

Through it all, over and over, He pointed their innocently confused faces to that third day when the depth and enormity of the temporary horror He'd marched willingly toward would be swallowed whole by the eternal magnificence He was destined to soar into.

Can you imagine that moment—in the darkness of the tomb? Heaven's clock ticks past the last ordained second, and hell's jubilee is yanked to a screeching halt.

How does life reenter a corpse that's been dead for three days? What happens first? The spirit returns, the heart fills with blood, the nerves reattach, and the decayed tissues reconstruct cell by cell, molecule by molecule? The more one tries to figure it out, the more bafflingly miraculous it all becomes.

In my imagination, I see stillness, engulfing blackness . . . a blackness so black; and silence . . . a silence so silent . . . the silence of death.

The lifeless flesh lies straight and flat and still—so incredibly still. Then in suddenness beyond suddenness, with a sound like a megaton implosion of atmosphere rushing into a sealed vacuum, the chest heaves heavenward in one massive, back-arching thrust as the breath of life reenters and blasts anew, exploding through the lungs with all the resurrection force of heaven and earth!

Like a rush of flood waters ripping outward from the chest to the limbs, tissues snap awake, muscles slam to attention, veins pop and ripple, bulging hard against the skin.

The left hand tenses and grips, the right follows suit, and in one blindingly deft and monumentally sweeping motion, the body hoists itself erect and rises to its feet, arms thrusting skyward like two mighty pistons in an unbridled explosion of magnificence that surpasses magnificence, victory that redefines victory, joy like there never has been joy!

Throwing His head back like a stallion, hair whipping in a thick, black mane, He trumpets an unbridled, eternity-altering cry of laughter and praise to the Father, and the infinite legions of heaven's created and heaven's Creator leap and whirl and roar right along with Him: "He lives! He lives! He is Jesus, and *He lives!*"

Remarkably, throughout Galilee and Judea and all the ancient world it appeared to be a day much like any other, that third day. We'd like to think it wasn't—maybe an unseasonable wisp of spring dancing on the breeze, the sun rising with an unusual sparkle. We'd like to think there was "something in the air" that day—something everyone felt—a tension of expectancy perhaps.

But the truth be told, it was a day like any other, much like the day He was first born. Farmers rose early and dragged their plows into the fields. Children ran giggling through the streets and alleyways. Wives and mothers gathered at the river to scrub yesterday's dirt off of tomorrow's clothes. The marketplaces buzzed with merchants and villagers, the roadways with chariots and donkey carts. Chickens were bought, goats were sold, dinner was cooked—

and the Son of the Living God rose from the dead.

He would tell them to

no longer cling to

Him but instead turn

their hearts toward

the next part of His

Father's plan—His

Spirit in theirs.

Take what I've given you and change the world.

There are so many mysteries revolving around it all. Why did no one recognize Him on sight? One of His dearest friends thought He was a gardener, and two of His disciples trekked miles alongside Him without a clue.

Why did He suddenly start walking through doors instead of knocking on them? Why did He still have the nail holes in His hands and the spear gash in His side? Why, why, why? . . .

There have been a multitude of explanations and analyses, but the bottom line is the bottom line: No one really has the slightest idea. He is God, and who can fathom His ways?

But for me, the greatest mysteries are not so much those "spiritual" things, but more the practical, behavioral things. It astounds me, for example, that of all the "biggies" He could have first revealed Himself to—the apostles John or Peter, His mother—He chose one who was more than likely an ex-prostitute, Mary of the town of Magdala, a woman left out by the "righteous" ones, laughed at by the world.

It astounds me, the things He chose *not* to do. He didn't march up the stairs of the Roman governor's palace—the man who'd handed Him over to be killed—and call him out in front of the masses. He didn't pay the priests and teachers of the law the little visit they surely deserved. He didn't fly through the air surrounded by angels and land in the temple court and shout to the world, "I told you so!"

Instead, He quietly visited His family and friends. He talked to them and he showed them His wounds. He cooked for them, helped them in their work, assured them, counseled them, ate with them, pointed them to the future; and in keeping with every moment He'd spent with them in the previous couple of years, He quite simply and breathtakingly—loved them.

There would be no earthly hoopla. There would be no triumphant reception, no victory parade, no first-century press conference, no celebrations. Mysteriously, remarkably, shockingly, unfathomably, Jesus played it all in the exact same way He'd played everything that had gone before—that way that is so mind-bendingly opposite ours—subtle, simple, soft-spoken, gentle, guileless, low-key, forgiving, kind, backseat. *Jesus.*

And when He was confident they understood, certain they could stand on their own feet and march forward into the adventures He'd been preparing them for all along, He would leave them. He would tell them to no longer cling to Him but instead turn their hearts toward the next part of His Father's plan—His Spirit in theirs, filling them, cleansing them, equipping them, leading them, guiding them, loving them—being Him to them and for them, within them.

He would march them up a mountainside to a peak where they had probably sat at His feet countless times—these fishermen, thieves, prostitutes—these seeming nobodies. He would turn to them and share a final word: "Take what I've given you and change the world."

He would look each of them deeply in the soul—one long, last look. He would smile at each of them deeply in their hearts—one huge, loving smile. He would lift His gaze toward His Father, and before their very eyes, He would disappear behind the clouds and into the eternity from which He most assuredly came.

> *Peace I leave with you; My peace I give you . . .*
> *Do not let your hearts be troubled and*
> *do not be afraid.*
>
> *Remain in My love.*
>
> *And surely I am with you always,*
> to the very end of the age.

Jesus

Peace I leave with you;

My peace I give you . . .

And surely I am with you always,

to the very end of the age.

YESTERDAY,

That My joy

may be in you,

and that your joy

may be complete.

TODAY, AND FOREVER

chapter eight

Rest for your soul...

I can't imagine that any work with regard to Jesus would be complete without a summons to that which was what He and His life, His death, and His resurrection, were all about.

It is astounding, the choices of the Son of God. He stepped out of heavenly splendor and relinquished His every right as deity to assume the posture of an ordinary man; to walk among us and work with us; to taste our sorrows and celebrate our joys; to instruct us, lead us, heal us, reveal His Father's heart for us, and more than anything else, to die, opening the gateways of heaven to us.

And the big question about it all—the revelation question—is why? Why would the Son of the Living God, with all the options in the universe, make those kinds of choices?

I've answered that question many times in the preceeding pages. But it is so huge an answer—so desperately vital to grip and grasp and cling to and never let go of—that as much as I've said it and as much as you've probably heard it, it just can't be said or heard enough:

He loves you.

Just as you are, whoever you are, wherever you are—

He loves you.

You see, the Word of God is very clear: "All have sinned and fall short of the glory of God" (that means you and I and everyone else are exactly the same), and "the wages of sin is death." In dying as He did, Jesus paid those wages for you and for me, for all eternity. He offers that to us—to accept His self-sacrifice as full payment, free of charge, free for the asking, the free gift of eternal life.

And so my question to you is, have you received this gift? Only you and He know, and if you haven't, I can promise you that He's offering it to you in the privacy of your own heart right now as you read these words.

Jesus said, "Here I am! I stand at the door and knock." Is He knocking on the door of your heart? Won't you let Him in?